METATRON'S 21-DAY MEDITATION CHALLENGE WORKBOOK

DEBBRA LUPIEN

Lupien Limited

Lupien Limited

Cresco, PA 18326

Cover image Image by 🌸 🌻 from Pixabay

Metatron's Cube by Nicolás Damián Visceglio from Pixabay

Voice of the Akashic Records, Book 3

Metatron's 21-Day Meditation Challenge Workbook/ Debbra Lupien — 1st ed.

Library of Congress Control Number: 2021922937

ISBN 978-0-9994880-5-8 (Kindle)

ISBN 978-0-9994880-6-5 (Paperback)

Note From The Author

This workbook is meant to be used with *The Path to Hearing Angels & Guides* book. If you haven't already gotten that book, I highly recommend starting there for context.

Introduction

When Metatron *strongly* suggested I host the 21-Day Meditation challenge before publishing *The Path to Hearing Angels & Guides*, I planted my feet and said no, it was premature. The book had to come first.

My resistance didn't last long because Metatron can be quite persuasive and I've never known him to be wrong. So it was that I opened the doors with a pre-launch version of the book and the challenge was off to the races. (You'll find that conversation in the book if you haven't already discovered it.)

I opened the support group a week before the challenge was scheduled to begin. During that week the wisdom of doing it Metatron's way was immediately evident.

The importance of a beta group to shake out the kinks and prove the concept cannot be overstated.

The beta run also presented an opportunity for Metatron to send daily messages, which were also invaluable. He doesn't do things half way!

Now as *you* begin your own 21-day challenge, you have a framework, more tools, and more support, because of those who have gone before and Metatron lobbying on your behalf.

Those daily messages have been compiled into this workbook where you'll benefit from their wisdom as you show up each day of the challenge. It's also the place to record your experience, because that's vitally important.

So let the challenge begin, and please do share your thoughts, questions, and ahas in the support group. Not only will *you* benefit, but others will as well. Just as you will benefit from having access to the same from other participants.

The march towards Earthtopia is underway and we'll all get there sooner by marching together.

Wishing you a transformational, ultra-satisfying 21 days and beyond.

Love and blessings,

Debbra

You'll find all the links mentioned herein at: https://Akasha-Unleashed.com/lightworkers-path

Challenge Day 1

Metatron: Blessings to you dear soul for accepting the challenge to more fluidly commune with your angels and guides. They are weeping and dancing with joy in anticipation of a new, deeper connection where they might be of greater service to you.

This is a loving, empowering, commitment to yourself. We are here to support you. Give yourself the grace of flowing with ease through this challenge. Select a time for your 15-minute meditation that works best for you. Try to eliminate as many distractions as possible.

Let go of any pre-conceived notions about what the experience *should* be and allow it to organically evolve.

Be kind to yourself.

You can't do it wrong. Feel your way through to a meditation practice that fits you and your lifestyle. In the beginning (*and this is vitally important*), do not force yourself to extend the time. Fifteen minutes is sufficient.

The exception would be if you're in the middle of receiving a message, allow it to continue. Otherwise stick to fifteen minutes, lest you sabotage your efforts with early over enthusiasm. This is not a sprint, it is a marathon. Slow and steady will help you reach your goals faster and easier than you ever imagined.

Do ask for help from your Akashic team, or your third-dimensional support group, and do share your experience with others if you feel comfortable doing so. (Consider sharing even if you feel uncomfortable, because it's a growth opportunity.) It is safe to share within your group, and it is excellent practice in overcoming old fears that have kept you hiding your brilliant light from the world.

Tell others outside your group about this experience so that more may choose to join in the quest to promote transformative change. There is power in numbers. As the very Earth beneath your feet shifts, presenting extraordinary challenges, the need for lightworkers to join together for the purpose of grand transformation is critical. Each and every one of you play a vital role in writing a new chapter for humanity and Earth.

Remember: flow and ease, along with deep belly breaths, as you use the *breathe, relax, allow* mantra to focus and make the connection with your angels and guides.

Please refrain from self judgment and criticism. That is counter productive. Speak loving, encouraging words to yourself and those around you. Remember they are also divine souls on a spiritual journey — equally loved by Creator.

Allow the deep love your Creator has for *you* to fill you to overflowing and then share that love with the world. Love is the answer. Love conquers all. Love is the most powerful force in the multiverse and *you* have an endless supply from which to draw.

Our deepest love, admiration, and respect for you Dear One. For in this time of need you found the courage and chose to answer the call of your Creator, honoring the commitment you made before embarking upon this present incarnation.

We, your team, stand in solidarity with you each step of the way. You will *never* be alone. Call upon us every minute of every day and we pledge to be there, for nothing is too great to ask. Thy will be done.

So it is and so it shall be unto eternity. Forever and ever amen.

CONSIDER JOINING THE FACEBOOK SUPPORT GROUP (if you haven't already). The transformation potential is vast. Support will magnify your experience. (Link p. 135)

Day 1 Journal

Challenge Day 2

Metatron: First: congratulations for the progress you have made. No matter whether it was one step or 10 steps, forward momentum is forward momentum. This we acknowledge and celebrate.

If you have posted about your experience in the support group, we salute you. Sharing posts are a delight to your team. They beam with joy at your enthusiasm.

If you do not choose to share we acknowledge and celebrate you also. Showing up, reading the posts, adding your energy is important.

Everything means something, nothing means nothing.

Just as we have long encouraged *you* to celebrate the tiniest steps of progress, so too do *we* celebrate any and all progress. We know that once you get moving in the right direction you will build momentum.

We promise you that any effort you make to connect with your team will bear many times more fruit than the effort you put forth. Now is a pivotal time in your journey.

This is your opportunity to get ahead of the curve by doing the preparatory work, rather than waiting until you're in the midst of the great shift.

Think of it like going to the gym to work out and build your muscles so that you'll be ready for heavy lifting when the time comes.

You have been preparing for this time over many lifetimes. You *are* ready for the most satisfying life experience up to this point. Put aside doubt and fear. Trust your team to help you navigate the difficult terrain ahead. When you lean on us it will be a veritable piece of cake.

Allow yourself to have some small wins (such as completing your 15-minute meditation each day), because those small wins all stacked up together amount to a sizable win that will leave you with more clarity and confidence as you prepare for the next phase of your transformational journey.

Copious amounts of joy, wonder, and delight await you just around the corner. With each small win you move closer and closer to that which you seek. One foot in front of the another, forward, ever forward. That's the way. Yes! Keep going.

We are with you, holding you up when you're weary, cheering when you feel discouraged, pointing to the light when you feel lost, celebrating each and every accomplishment.

You might say we are your *HELICOPTER** team, for we notice and respond to every breath, every thought, every need. It has always been thus. Now as your awareness expands you will see, hear, feel, and know this is Divine Truth. (*A reference to Helicopter moms who hover over their children.)

That delicious connection you have been seeking is yours for the having. Go ahead, turn up the volume. We'll wait.

.

Day 2 Journal

_____

_____

_____

_____

_____

_____

_____

_____

_____

_____

_____

_____

_____

_____

_____

_____

_____

_____

_____

_____

_____

_____

_____

_____

_____

_____

_____

_____

_____

_____

_____

Challenge Day 3

Metatron: We are most gratified to see the diligence you have been applying in this challenge. We realize it is a big ask, given the state of the world and economy. We're honored you choose to devote a small portion of your day with your faithful team.

Now that you are beginning to understand and feel comfortable with the challenge, we encourage you to lean even more into *allow and flow*. The most important takeaway for you is the fluidity of connection. That is the muscle we are helping you tone.

There will be time enough to connect for the purpose of asking specific questions. Not that we are opposed to answering anything you wish to ask, however, that should not be your first priority. Number one is developing your ability to connect and hear your team with ease and confidence that you are, in fact, receiving Divine messages.

Notice how much easier it has been when you play this *game* with others? Yes, game. Always remember to interject fun into your day. It is a vital ingredient in your long-term success.

One day you will easily connect at will while you go about your day; flowing in and out of conversation with your team. Never worry about conversations being interrupted. Simply pick up where you left off when you are able to reconnect. It's not so different from momentarily putting your phone on hold.

As you go about your day, pause once in a while to express love and gratitude to yourself, and your Creator, for this experience and your role in it. *Gratitude will shift your energy in the most marvelous way, opening the door to even more flow.*

Because of your commitment many others will benefit, both directly and indirectly. Never lose sight that you as an individual play a vital role in the larger cosmic story. Without you it would be incomplete. With you, it is all the sweeter and more full bodied, like an excellent wine.

Delight in all that you are and all that you have and it will expand. *You* will expand, one glorious step at a time.

That is enough for this day.

Until the 'morrow we bid you adieu.

Day 3 Journal

_____

_____

_____

_____

_____

_____

_____

_____

_____

_____

_____

DEBBRA LUPIEN

Challenge Day 4

Metatron: Superlative efforts! We are over the moon tickled to witness your dedication and commitment. You have already surpassed our expectations and that's not hyperbole.

Can you hear us cheering you on?

There are volumes that we wish to share with you. This is just the warm-up period. Keep moving forward as you have and you will amaze even yourself.

Let us know what you need from us to support your efforts. Of course we know what you need, but it's important for you to articulate because your opinion may perhaps be different from ours. That opens the door to a deeper conversation and an opportunity for you to stretch a little bit out of your comfort zone as you make the effort to reach up to meet our outstretched hands.

Never be afraid to reach for the stars. We will boost you up, or send winged angels to transport you. If it's your desire, a way will be made. Leave the heavy lifting up to us.

You are like the head chef dreaming up delectable creations. We are your sous chefs attending to the nitty gritty details. 😊 And you have *many* sous chefs! We're not talking average run of the mill creations, we're talking top of the line gourmet all the way baby! Only the best will do for you.

The only limits are the ones you place upon yourself. We challenge you to release them one by one until you are free to expand in any direction you choose.

Today we encourage you to show more love, respect, and appreciation for yourself.

YOU are a marvel.

YOU made the commitment to your spiritual growth.

YOU are lining up breakthrough after breakthrough for yourself.

Talk about manifesting on steroids! When you partner with your team it's in the bag.

(Hearing: *Jumping Jack Flash* it's a gas, gas, gas... (Link p. 135))

Sing it baby! Sing it out loud. Own it! You've got this! 🩶

P.S. Go ahead and dance if you want to we'll dance right along with you.

Lots of love. See ya on the flip side.

Day 4 Journal

_____

_____

_____

_____

_____

_____

_____

_____

_____

_____

_____

Challenge Day 5

Metatron: Things are falling into place just as we anticipated.

You have done well. Tomorrow you will do even better. Each day you build upon the last in confidence, clarity, and probably most important: patience.

You are in the midst of a transformation unlike any you have yet experienced. That does not mean that your transformation will look like a fellow participant's. Remember: comparing one's unique self to another will lead you down the garden path, so to speak.

While gardens are lovely, that is not the path we are focused on at the moment.

If you want to assess your progress, check in with your solar plexus. How does it feel? That is your handy/dandy built-in barometer with which to measure such things.

There may be some days when you feel as if you're losing ground, slipping backwards. We assure you that is not true, and is but another of those pesky illusions that so often trip you up.

Just as your physical muscles need time to recover after a new workout, so too does your psyche. You are moving forward at an accelerated pace so that when a necessary *pause to catch up day* happens, it may feel like you slammed on the brakes and gave yourself whiplash.

Rather than feel discouraged, we say celebrate for you wouldn't need a pause if you weren't making stellar progress.

Keep your eyes focused on the horizon ahead, one step at a time move forwards towards your goal of successfully completing this challenge.

Give yourself a pep talk, if need be. Know that the truth of the matter is you are doing *splendidly*. Do not fall into the trap of telling yourself otherwise. Don't fall for the lies of ego, who means well, but is wholly ineffective when it comes to consciousness expansion.

Don't forget to occasionally review your journal for the ahas and breakthroughs. They are proof of your progress and will give you a much-needed boost at those times you feel low.

Understand highs and lows are a natural part of the journey. If you only had highs they would soon lose their appeal. Lows are an important contrast so that the highs will feel all the sweeter.

Just as tide waters ebb and flow, so too do you. It's a natural rhythm, it's energy in motion, it's flow and ease. They are all connected.

Those energy cycles are present all over Creation, always at play, much like the inner workings of a clock. You might say energy cycles are the *gears of life*.

It's when energy slows or shuts down that you need to sit up and take notice. Figure out where the blockage is, clear it ASAP and resume your flow once more.

Periodically checking in on your flow is wise so that you might make minor course corrections along the way. That is a far more pleasant journey than allowing yourself to get far off course, where it may require a figurative *act of God* to turn things around.

Make this regular checking in a part of your self-care routine, for it *is* the ultimate in self care.

Your highest responsibility is to yourself. You've been given one skin suit for the duration of this incarnation, so give it the best care while you're expanding your consciousness. They go hand in hand.

And now, we'll leave you to ponder these thoughts until we connect once again tomorrow.

Rest well Dear One.

Day 5 Journal

_____
_____
_____
_____
_____
_____
_____
_____
_____
_____
_____

_____

_____

_____

_____

_____

_____

_____

_____

_____

_____

_____

_____

_____

_____

_____

_____

_____

_____

_____

_____

_____

Challenge Day 6

There's a buzzing sound like busy little bees. Very industrious little bees!

Metatron: Sometimes too much buzzing obfuscates the message transmission.

When you *graduate* to the place where you can tame that buzzing, the underlying message will seep through. This takes longer for some than others. There is no judgment on our part with regard to your timing. We urge you to refrain from judging self lest it discourage and sidetrack your progress.

Remember, there is no one like you, therefore, no one to whom you can compare.

Should you notice this buzzing situation, make note of the details, down to the tiniest. It's something!

On those days when it feels as if you got zero, bupkis, nothing, look for the subtle notes that linger like a fine perfume. They are always there, even though it may take more scrutiny than normal to discover and appreciate them.

Allow yourself to savor the fragrance, run it through your chakras, and notice whether you feel any difference in the energy signature.

Does it flow equally well through each chakra, or is it stickier in one than another? Notate these details as they will be important in unlocking the secret to a more fluid, flowing connection.

Is it a familiar feeling? Are you aware of it showing up previously? How does it make you feel? What does it inspire?

As you experience the subtle energy passing through each chakra, make note of any variation in what you feel. These are tiny clues that may have significant impact.

Once you start noticing the tiniest of clues, you will notice more significant clues showing up. Things that were likely there all along, but you had not yet fine tuned *the frequency* to receive.

When you connect with your guides, it is very much like finding your favorite channel on the radio. Over time, you will learn to feel your way through the subtle shifts to reach a deeper, clearer connection sooner.

If you fail to precisely tune the channel, you can expect to feel frustrated. Much as some reported feeling disappointed when their fingers slipped out of place while typing, resulting in gobbledygook which they are unable to translate.

In actuality it would be possible to translate as you map out which letters shifted and then convert them back into aligned letters, although that is a lot of bother.

While this is surely frustrating it is not that uncommon. Most of you do not regularly type with your eyes closed, so there's no reason to expect you can do so immediately and expertly.

Know that it's perfectly fine to open your eyes to check your finger placement and typed words. You merely pause your meditation for a moment, realign your fingers, then close your eyes again, take a few deep breaths and ask that the message resume. (Feeling for the ridges on the F and J keys will help keep you on track.)

It may feel jarring at first, but like most things, with practice it will be seamless and simple. This is an excellent skill to develop as during meditation the potential for all manner of distractions exists. Now you'll pick right back up where you left off with barely a bauble. We hope that excites you as much as it does us.

Debbra: What wisdom will you share with those who are frustrated at not hearing or seeing anything yet?

Metatron: Be kind to yourself. You are like a babe who has only just begun. Allow yourself the space to find the most comfortable and effective way to connect. Know that your way may look and sound entirely different from others. No worries about doing it *wrong*. In actuality there is NO wrong way. There's simply doing what feels best, flowing with it, then allowing inspiration and curiosity to assist in your forward momentum.

It's that self judgment and disappointment that will grind your progress to a halt. Accept that you are doing your best and that is always enough. There are no taskmasters standing over you with a whip (other than yourself).

Lovingly support your own efforts in testing and tweaking to find the most effective, most comfortable path. We will more than meet you halfway.

Signing off. Transmission ended.

Day 6 Journal

_____

_____

_____

_____

_____

_____

_____

_____

_____

_____

_____

Challenge Day 7

Debbra: Today I was inspired to look up the symbolism of 7.

Angel Number 7 tells of a beneficial time with obstacles overcome and successes realized. Your angels are happy with your life choices and are telling you that you are currently on the right path. You are encouraged to keep up the good work you have been doing as you are successfully serving your soul purpose and life mission and your angels are supporting you all the way. Positive things will flow freely towards you, and this will assist you along your journey.

Angel Number 7 suggests that you look to further developing your personal spirituality and encourage others to do the same. Angel Number 7 tells of learning new skills, listening to your own inner-knowing, and stepping out of your comfort zone in order to further develop and advance on all levels. You have an important soul mission and life purpose that involves communicating, teaching and healing others and serving humanity in a manner that suits you best. You are encouraged to set a positive example for others and inspire them to seek their own passion and purpose in life.

Angel Number 7 also encourages you to take up a spiritually-based practice, profession and/or career or heart-based service if you are so inclined.

METATRON: AS WE BRING WEEK ONE TO A CLOSE, allow yourself a little more ease and flow. Rest is a vitally important component in your recipe for success.

Reflect, refuel, refresh, rejuvenate. Allow all that you have experienced to wash over you and as it does, notice should any of the pieces suddenly fit together in a way you had not before recognized.

A deeper meaning* may reveal itself now or it may one day soon. Either is perfect. Your assignment is to be present. Know that the day will come when your world expands and you'll suddenly have greater awareness of everything.

When that day arrives, your energy, along with your perception of self and the world will shift. That's the cycle you have entered: Forward progress, pause, assess, allow new understanding to become a part of you, rest, repeat the cycle.

Vision: Driving your car up one of those circular airport garages. Round and round and round, level out as you approach the next level, then begin again.

Metatron: That is all for this day. Brevity is called for to allow processing time. Remember to express gratitude for yourself and your team. Bask in appreciation for what you have accomplished (no matter how small it may feel), for it's a part of upleveling your vibrational frequency.

Know that your team and I are pleased to accompany you on this journey and delight in your expansion.

Namasté Dear Child

* DEEPER MEANINGS DID EMERGE FOR MANY participants who experienced revelations and peeling away layers of old *stuff* to allow healing to occur.

Day 7 Journal

_____

_____

_____

_____

_____

_____

_____

_____

_____

_____

_____

_____

Challenge Day 8

Metatron: We salute you for your diligence. For staying the course, soldiering on, even though at times you might have felt discouraged or even defeated.

Our promise and commitment to you is that we will be with you every step of the journey, helping in whatever way you allow. Don't forget to ask for anything you need.

Keep leaning into more lightness and levity. That will serve you well as you delve even deeper in this, the second week, of your challenge.

The ability to maintain a sense of humor and not take things so seriously is key and will serve you in good stead.

Remember should you feel stuck, you can always insert your own visualization to *prime the pump*. If you lack for creative ideas, perhaps a lively game of volleyball on the beach with your angel team?

You can dream up anything that feels good. That's the raw material, we'll work with, and fashion messages from that jumping off place.

Just as in a conversation there is give and take between the parties, so too is there give and take in your meditative messages. You may begin or allow us to begin, whichever works best for you.

While you might think the ideas you come up with are random, can you really be sure? 😊 What if we told you we had a hand in influencing those *random* thoughts?

You see, you can't get it wrong.

Breathe, relax, allow, kick things off with your own images if you choose. The important thing is to have a positive interaction. No self recriminations or self judgment. Just flow and allow the experience to evolve.

Some days the perfect thing is to just sit quietly observing your breathing. Those are natural lulls in your expansion, every bit as important as the fanciful imagery.

This bears repeating: *everything means something, nothing means nothing.*

You are becoming more tuned into your physical body as well as your ethereal one. Both are important. Shifts you have yet to become aware of in the now will be as obvious as the nose on your face tomorrow, or the next day, or the next.

Tune in, tap in, and trust the process. It has been carefully crafted to facilitate your expansion and joyful transformation. This is not our first rodeo. 😊

We are, of course, being playful with you to demonstrate how easy your experience can be.

We've been showing up 24/7 for you lo these many years (and lifetimes.) You have no idea how elated we are for the tiniest baby steps forward. And you've arrived right on time as the prophecy of Earthtopia*, the very reason you are on the planet at this time, draws near fulfillment.

You, yes *YOU* are a vital component in the grand plan. Very much needed and appreciated. We love your enthusiasm and eagerness. We raise you a healthy portion of peace. (Yes, we did just use a poker analogy!) Got your attention, right?

You are perfectly situated to move into week 2 and all the wondrous marvels yet to be revealed. Onward in peace, love and joy into your glorious, abundant tomorrow!

We'll catch you on the flip side. LOL

*Learn more about the prophecy of Earthtopia (link p. 135).

Day 8 Journal

_____

_____

_____

_____

_____

_____

_____

_____

_____

_____

_____

Challenge Day 9

Metatron: Nine* fold is auspicious.

For all who have ears to hear, whether you are actively participating daily, or whether you're dabbling, you are loved, supported, and encouraged.

Your team stands ready to accompany you on the journey *YOU* choose. It has always been thus and will always be.

Sometimes you bite off more than you can chew. In those moments it is wise to pause, reflect and then decide what is in your highest and best interests. That applies to this challenge and to *everything* in your life.

We wish to impart to you how very important stepping into the power of choice is on your journey.

Each choice is like a little jet pack that propels you forward. As it winds down, more choices come into your awareness.

Look them over and choose the very best to refuel your little jet pack as you surge forward once more. Your choices function like a rudder influencing the direction that you travel.

Understand, you needn't wait until the last surge is over, or nearly so, before making the next choice. In fact should you make choices faster, you needn't slow at all. Maintain your momentum with more and varied choices, savoring the deliciousness of the journey along the way as you flow from one choice to the next.

When you choose this as your way of being, you will find there is more joy and excitement, along with an abundance of love. You will be so filled with love as you glide forth on your purposeful path that love will flow out of your very pores. It will have substance and depth. It *will* be felt.

If you were to fly above the clouds, you could seed them with love, which would then rain down upon the world, spreading massive waves of love across the land. That is the power and vastness available to you when you function from a place of alignment.

Lest you think this is hyperbole, let us remind you that *YOU* are a powerful creator in your own right. When you're in the flow and "jet propelled" by love, you can change the world. Your energy and intent surge out in front, paving the way for miracles.

From this place of alignment anything is possible. As you step up to the plate from this new, expanded, powerful way of being, it is now time to focus on being more specifically intentional.

When you're just learning a new skill, as you have been for the past 8 days, there is more space and less specificity — like traveling on a wide road. However, in this process you have been raising your vibrational frequency, which means the road has narrowed, requiring more precision and more specificity.

A higher level of responsibility is now called for. Double down on being more present in every moment, take inspired action sooner as you level up into even greater possibilities.

You may have heard the phrase: to whom much is given, much is expected. There is truth in that statement.

What's missing from that equation is that it is you who have given this higher level of responsibility, and thus creation ability, to yourself. You have worked your way up to this place through focus, determination, and dedication. Savor your accomplishments, and give yourself due credit.

It's perfectly fine to pause or idle (like a motor vehicle), for a bit as you allow yourself to feel your way into this new version of you.

When you are ready for more, just say the word. We'll be right here waiting to help you launch into the stratosphere of even more amazing possibilities.

Remember it is up to you to set the pace. Slow down, speed up, or idle a bit, it's totally up to you. Choose what feels best and know *that* is the right choice.

Release the need to second guess or judge. Where you are is perfect for you. Celebrate who and where you are in this moment, and in every moment. You have already come very far and it is our delight to witness and assist.

Your progress in this particular lifetime far surpasses what you have previously experienced. This time is different. You had loftier goals and you requested that we step up *our* game to nudge where needed and help keep you on track. So if you've felt more urgency this time around that is why.

We are stepping up our efforts, just as you requested, and we can affirm for you that you *are* on track with your vision and plan. Yes there is more expansion ahead, that is always true. But in this moment you are on target to meet, and likely exceed, your stated goals.

We could go on and on extolling your many virtues and accomplishments. But for now it is prudent to pause and allow you to process what we have shared.

Go forth in love and light, feeling your way through the day, expecting and accepting miracles, because they are the fruits of your manifesting labors.

THE DEFINITION OF NINEFOLD DIDN'T particularly connect to the message, so I turned to angel numbers for a clue. Oh yeah, pay dirt!

ANGEL NUMBER 9 IS A SIGN FROM THE ANGELS THAT your life path and soul mission involve being of service to humanity through the use of your natural skills and talents.

Angel Number 9 suggests that you are a natural lightworker and encourages you to look to ways to serve others in positively uplifting ways.

Angel Number 9 may be indicating that it is time to end a phase, situation or relationship that is no longer serving you in a positive way. Rest assured that 'new' will enter your life that will enhance and benefit your life and lifestyle in many ways. Prepare yourself today as there is much work for you to do.

Angel Number 9 encourages you to be compassionate, thoughtful, philanthropic and of service to others, and humanity as a whole, as you lead others by positive example.

Day 9 Journal

_____

_____

_____

_____

_____

_____

_____

_____

_____

_____

_____

_____

_____

_____

_____

_____

_____

_____

_____

_____

_____

_____

_____

_____

_____

_____

_____

_____

_____

Challenge Day 10

Metatron: There is a great deal more to say and teach, however, when making such rapid progress it is important to pause now and again to allow new understanding and creative insights to be fully absorbed.

New concepts and ideas race through the neurons of your brain, lighting up all the dark corners, inspiring new perspective and action. Sometimes it's a veritable pin-ball machine in your head. Allow the game to run its course as you digest the lessons thus far imparted.

Replay the best parts, the ones that really light you up. Savor the most delicious bits. Then digest your scrumptious *gourmet meal*, taking time to bask in gratitude for what you have received, and for your own efforts in this endeavor.

Never lose sight of the truth that it is due to your own commitment and fortitude that you have come so far. Know that same grit will carry you much further still.

Fortified and sufficiently nourished, step right up to the front of the line as you prepare to continue your journey, full steam ahead.

What is your desire for the next leg of this journey? Set your intentions now and your team will step up to home plate preparing for a grand slam that will deliver all you asked and more. (Yes, now baseball analogies.)

Your team is just getting warmed up and are ready to dazzle you. They've waited so long for this opportunity and plan to take full advantage, so hold onto your hat as they rev up the engines and shift right up into overdrive. Woowee it's going to be a ride to remember!

Now we realize you may be on fire to keep charging forward, but a pause is prudent. Much like a race car must make periodic pit stops for maintenance and safety checks, so too is it wise for you to take advantage of your ebbs to do a thorough check. Is your engine firing on all cylinders or is there a bit of knocking going on?

Maybe you've been burning a bit too much midnight oil, or not getting sufficient sunlight and fresh air? This is your opportunity to do your own safety checks before getting back out on that track and burning rubber.

Remember to pace yourself so that you don't *run out of gas* prematurely. You have all the resources necessary at your disposal, courtesy of your team, but you must ask. They cannot interfere. Should you get depleted and wait too long to request their help, you may set your progress back as you are forced to take a longer break until you have sufficiently topped off your energy tanks before continuing.

Tempering your enthusiasm while planning the route to success is a wise choice.

We honor and salute you magnificent soul. Love, light, and gratitude today and always. (Your team fades out to Kool and The Gang singing Celebration (Link p. 135))

Day 10 Journal

_____

_____

_____

_____

_____

_____

_____

_____

_____

_____

_____

Challenge Day 11

Metatron: Breathe, relax, allow. Find your peaceful point and abide. Allow peace to permeate your every cell. Flow into and through peace. In this moment there is *only* peace.

Let peace be your focus for this day. No regrets, recriminations, or pushing through for bigger, better. Just *be the peace* you wish to share with the world.

Feel peace emanating from you into the ether, joining with intentional peace sent from like-minded lightworkers. Watch it expand into a ginormous bubble of peace that floats up and over the planet, seeding the clouds with peace pods to rain down upon the land.

This collective *Peace Process* will soften resistance and beckon those who thirst for something better, more fulfilling. They may not understand what it is, but they will be curious and drawn to seek out more so that they might understand what this peculiar experience is all about.

As they allow themselves to step into the path of peace energy it will permeate *their* every cell, further softening that hard outer layer of resistance.

As peace integrates with their third-dimensional awareness it will cause them to shift. Some will respond faster and more positively than others. No matter as this process will be repeated.

You may send more peace energy as you feel led. Over time, more and more will feel called to join as you move towards the point of critical mass.

Had you gone forth into battle to defeat those opposed to peace, you would have engaged in two-way resistance. Far better to send out peace bubbles and allow them to do the work. You can accomplish more with energetic intent than you can in a resistant state with sticks and knives.

Allow the opponents of peace to come around in their own time so that they feel it was their idea and are willing, enthusiastic even, to get on board the *Peace Process* movement.

In this way you will simply flow into critical mass as more and more new converts happily join your (now their), cause.

You will be victorious, having won without resistance. Yes, your angels in their beautiful armor stand side by side ready to fight alongside you, but remember: it is a psychic battle; it is a peaceful battle. No matter how much an oxymoron that seems.

You are sending out the energy; they are responding out of curiosity because it's not what they expected. They will have been converted before they even realize they're being wooed by the *Peace Process*.

When Divine turns on the charm and woos, resistance is futile in the very best way.

Together let us send out the call to all lightworkers: put on your armor so that you might feel strengthened and confident, link arms with your angels, prepare for battle, then collectively let loose with a massive volley of peace energy, and intention.

Vision: A catapult being used to launch your beautiful, sparkling, peace bubble. Then an entire line of catapults launching volley after volley.

Metatron: When all the peace energy has been dispatched, revert to your breathe, relax, allow mantra. Celebrate the wave of peace that even now grows into a tidal wave to end all tidal waves. This is the cosmic wave of transformation*, ready to deliver its payload across the land.

The transmission is complete.

* METATRON HAS BEEN REFERENCING THE COSMIC Wave of Transformation since 2017. (Link p. 135)

Day 11 Journal

_____

_____

_____

_____

_____

_____

_____

_____

_____

_____

_____

Challenge Day 12

Metatron: You have created a solid foundation upon which to build. A stellar achievement! Some are now ready to build up, while others will want to further expand their foundation. Either is fine. Choose which feels best.

It is natural and expected that you would move forward at vastly different pacing one from another. Do not compare yourself to anyone. Your perfect progress is your priority. Allow it to unfold in your personal Divine timing.

At this milestone it would be appropriate to pause in gratitude for what you've accomplished and what is to come.

If you have reached day 12, it means you have steadfastly persisted, and are poised for further expansion. Doors are even now opening for you. New opportunities of all sorts will soon be revealed. Be vigilant in watching for them so that you might take fast action and then bask in appreciation for the fruits of your labors.

Appreciating and basking are important components in your formula for success. They shift your energy ever higher so that you might have more wisdom, more insight, more love of self, and the world. For, as you bask and appreciate your magnificent self, the love energy will overflow and fan out to touch others.

Don't be in such a hurry that you skip the basking/appreciating part as it's an important energetic equalizer. Remember, balance in all things.

The wise choice is slow, steady progress. Rushing leads to omitting important steps and imbalance. It halts ascension (to higher vibrational frequencies), as you cannot effectively move forward in an unbalanced state, for that would set you on a course to ultimately crash.

Yes you can get by for a time uncontrollably rushing forward, getting further and further off course until you reach the outer edges and spin out. Somewhat like a space capsule hurtling back to Earth, off course, missing the re-entry window and subsequently burning up in the atmosphere. Ouch! You don't want to go there.

This is why we often remind you to be present in the moment so that you might make *tiny* course corrections sooner when they are easily rectified.

We understand that your life is filled with all manner of distractions making it challenging to stay present, however; you *are* capable of perfectly steering your vessel, even in uncharted waters, because we are with you and provide ongoing navigational assistance as needed.

When you're present in the moment, you receive our navigational relays nearly instantaneously. When you're not, life becomes more challenging. This is why we keep banging the drum of being present, and will continue to do so as often as necessary.

Now would be an excellent time to review your journal. Reflect back to the beginning.

What techniques have you incorporated that helped you successfully complete your daily meditation? What has tripped you up? What new insights have you experienced? What is working? What isn't? What tweaks might you make to experience more flow and ease?

Highlight and celebrate each win or breakthrough. Remember how far you have come, because there will be challenging days now and again. Having your wins handy to review is the fastest, easiest way to quickly move past challenges and get right back on track.

Truly you were a success as soon as you agreed to this challenge. Since then you have progressed in a myriad of ways, some you have yet to recognize. It is a marvel to behold and we celebrate with you each and every step of the way.

Namasté Dear One!

With love and appreciation, Your Akashic Team.

Day 12 Journal

_____

_____

_____

_____

_____

_____

_____

_____

_____

_____

_____

Challenge Day 13

Metatron: It's all about changes. Changes in you, your physicality, your frequency.

Changing your perspective, changing your outlook on life. Changing anything and everything to suit you and make your journey both more pleasurable and more purposeful. Lean into change, as you manifest a glorious life.

For you, we wish more love, more light, more fun and more flight. (Flights of fancy that is.) Lean into the delightful freedom of being fanciful. That lightness of being will serve you in good stead.

What do you desire to create? Really, stop to consider the most delightful manifestations that are on your heart. See them, feel them, delight in them, and watch them spring up like poppies in the field, plentiful and colorful.

Time to kick things up a notch and seriously contemplate what it is you hope to create today, tomorrow and the next day. Manifest purposefully and consciously rather than by happenstance.

You've got the power, you've got the rhythm, now flow into *creation at the speed of thought*. That is the ultimate experience which springs forth when you are in complete alignment with your glorious soul.

Sing, dance, play the harmonica, whatever turns you on and lights you up. Your team will join you in your celebration.

Imagine a *Tiptoe Through The Tulips** kind of day. Being present in the moment, having a multi-sensory experience, squealing in delight as all your senses light up like a pinball machine. (*Song by Tiny Tim (Link p. 135))

We understand you may not feel quite ready for that level of expression and that's ok. Our purpose is to give you a taste of what might be.

It's your journey. You get to fill in the blanks in the way that is most pleasing to you. We aim to entice and inspire you to reach for more.

Never settle. You are not the settling kind. Your soul craves more and you can have more. We want you to see the many and varied vistas that are already open to you, with more being created all the time. Your soul did not come to live a life of limitation.

If you can dream it, you can have it. Never put a cap on your dreams. Never settle for less than the whole enchilada. You are a naturally abundant being. That is the truth of who you are. You understand that with perfect clarity when you are not in a body.

You have now come to the time of the great awakening when you will remember more of who you are and of what you are capable.

It's time to stop hiding your light under a bushel. It's time to step out into the bright light, nay spotlight even, and reveal the magnificence you've kept hidden inside your skin suit.

If you're reminded of the movie *Cocoon*, you're getting the idea. It **is** something like that — except even more magnificent!

Allow yourself to embrace that image, that feeling. For just a moment *be* that glorious soul.

Savor the feeling. Expand into it. Imagine what your life would look and feel like were you to live as a soul all the time. That's the direction you're headed.

We wanted to give you a sneak peek and feel of what's on your horizon. Our aim is to tantalize and fascinate so that you might aim higher. It's time and you're ready. One baby step at a time so you don't scare yourself.

There's a higher level of joy, wonder, and delight yet to be experienced. Yes even in the midst of the coming battle for Earth. One does not exclude the other. That duality is available to you, and we are here to help you ascend into that way of being.

We have waxed eloquent long enough. For now, soak upon our words, allow them to percolate into your psyche, reflect upon them and then consider what new action you might take. Your destiny awaits.

Blessed be.

Day 13 Journal

_____

_____

_____

_____

_____

_____

_____

_____

_____

_____

_____

Challenge Day 14

Metatron: Today marks the two-thirds point of your journey in this challenge. How do you feel? Are you satisfied with your progress?

If you've fallen behind or are struggling, will you continue on or give up? Know that we will lovingly support whatever choice you make. You simply cannot do this wrong. Your choices are yours and, therefore, perfect for you.

If you need support, please ask. As you may have noticed (if you're in the support group), your fellow participants are enthusiastic and eager to help. This challenge is not an obligation. It is a gift to yourself.

When you begin your meditation each day, remember to bring your child-like excitement and curiosity. Flow through the experience. Make note of how you feel.

Each time you connect in this way you *are* making progress whether or not it's obvious. You are feeling your way into a deeper connection with your personal team, who are there to cheer you on and lift you up. Your efforts bring incredible joy to your team. Allow yourself to feel that joy, and their support, as it can make the difference between continuing or not.

Please refrain from comparing yourself to others, as there is no other like you. You're a one-of-a-kind masterpiece *designed* by Creator.

We offer a standing ovation for those who are experiencing breakthroughs; enjoying a connection perhaps more profound than you've ever experienced. Your previous efforts have led you to this place and time, and that's perfect for you.

We hope you'll allow yourself to be in gratitude, first for yourself (because *you* did this), and then for others who have been a part of your journey.

On those days when you perhaps thought you'd never connect, you persevered and here you are, flowing with ease into multi-sensory connections as you expand your consciousness.

For those in the middle who feel as if their progress comes in fits and starts, we say: focus on the starts rather than the fits. 😊 Any progress is good progress.

It's perfectly normal to move forward and then slip back a bit before moving forward once more. As is often observed: three steps forward, two steps back. Sometimes that is the most effective method of expansion.

Remember each soul is uniquely *wired*. Find what works for you, your personal recipe for success. Focus on the horizon ahead, and keep going.

Self recrimination, guilt, looking back in regret, are all a waste of time and energy. You can't change the past, you can only learn the lesson and move on. Let it go as you'd let go refuse. You no longer need it.

Refuse clutters your space and diverts your attention from your purposeful journey. Chuck it out and make space for new, exciting experiences that expand your consciousness. Now that's a gourmet recipe!

Only the best for you.

Savor it and allow it to nourish your soul so that you might further expand. Rinse and repeat. This is a never-ending cycle; one that you have been practicing over many lifetimes.

The difference this time is that you are accelerating the process so that you're expanding into higher-dimensional awareness. So much more awaits you on the ascension path.

Remember it's not a sprint, it's a marathon. You are making excellent progress just by showing up.

Now consider how you might stretch just a bit more. Is it being kinder to yourself? Mustering up the courage to share your experience, or asking for help? Maybe it's allowing yourself to see new truths that your team brings forth so that you might recognize the root cause of troublesome blocks.

The answer to any question you could ever ask exists in your Akashic Records. You are on the precipice of a new way of being as you interact with your Records and your team.

Now let us address the way information is delivered.

Very often you will notice that answers come in a format that may feel like some sort of secret code. You may feel frustrated, wondering why don't we speak in a plainer manner, one more easily understood.

If it were possible, know that we would. When it *is* possible we do speak plainly. However, more often, answering plainly would influence your choices. That we cannot do, and as your consciousness rises, you will one day realize that you wouldn't want that, for then you'd effectively be our puppet.

So what if it takes effort on your part to connect the dots and understand the message? Through this process you are learning and growing, evaluating choices, and determining your own destiny.

That will stand you in good stead as you ascend the frequency ladder gaining a greater understanding of yourself and the Universe.

Be a diligent, dedicated student. Create a routine that will allow you to consistently practice. Ground yourself regularly. Ask for and receive a refill of your vital force energy so that your vessel is always overflowing. Allow love for your divine soul to expand within until you are overflowing with love for humanity and the planet.

That's the target you're aiming for at this time in your soul journey. That is the powerful place of understanding from which you are best poised to take your place alongside your fellow lightworkers as you fulfill the prophecy of Earthtopia.

In the doing and being on that journey you will experience more love, peace, and fulfillment than you can yet imagine. This exquisite potentiality is just over your horizon. Does that sound like something worthy of extra focus and diligence?

We say you would not have said yes to this challenge unless your soul was already joyously committed.

There's one more vitally important point we must make: none of this means you abandon your own personal purpose and journey. That is first and foremost who and what you're about.

Earthtopia is an extra assignment that you signed on for in the past and have eagerly anticipated. This does not mean the two are mutually exclusive. Far from it, they complement each other quite well. We simply want to ensure that you always put *your* needs and *your* journey first, because as a sovereign soul that *is* your responsibility.

You are the captain of your soul ship and all that entails. We are here to serve as your crew, or in whatever capacity you require.

Aye, aye Cap'n, everything's ship shape and we're ready to set sail upon your command. Over and out.

Day 14 Journal

_____

_____

_____

_____

_____

_____

_____

_____

_____

_____

Challenge Day 15

Metatron: As you begin the final week of this challenge, pause and take a look back at where you began. It's important to periodically contrast and compare as a measure of your progress.

You have already shifted far more than you know and are not the same person as when you started. Reviewing your journal now will encourage and fortify you as you head down the home stretch towards the finish line.

We encourage you to remain neutral regarding expectations, as results of week three may vary widely. You may have amazing new clarity and insights, or you may feel as if you've stalled. That's the nature of ebb and flow. Your rhythm will be different from your neighbor's. Yours is best for you.

Just keep showing up every day, doing the work, and your efforts will be rewarded. Remember, it takes time to build new muscles. Give yourself the grace to take the time it takes.

You may have wondered what happens after the challenge concludes? That is entirely up to you. Should you wish to continue your daily practice (and share in the group), please do. We would suggest you put away the daily timer and allow your daily meditation to run its natural course, if that's possible given your schedule.

Some participants have reported their meditation naturally wraps up in the allotted time. If you'd like to extend the time, you may need to set your intention to allow for that possibility.

Choose what feels best for you and do that, allowing details to change as you shift into a more deeply connected way of being.

Now that you've found a comfortable framework for your daily meditation, we encourage you to experiment. Put away preconceived notions about what *should* be and feel into what's the most satisfying, empowering method for you.

Never forget *you* are in charge. We are here to serve your needs today and every day of your lives.

Be mindful of flow and ease. Do not try to force. If you find a door that you struggle to open, it's either not your door or it's the wrong timing. Let it go and move on. Everything falls into place in Divine timing.

You have made excellent progress thus far and we salute you. Now it's time to shift into high gear, using everything you've learned, and cruise smoothly through the final week.

Love, light and kisses from your angels who delight in your triumphs and happiness.

Day 15 Journal

_____

_____

_____

_____

_____

_____

_____

_____

_____

_____

Challenge Day 16

Metatron: There is a warm feeling growing within us as we witness your expansion and dedication. A joy to behold.

A high-potency-energetic beam of love and appreciation streams from your team to you, forging an enduring and powerful connection.

Some days you may be acutely aware of this energy, while others you may forget all about it. Regardless, it will remain. Supporting, stimulating, soothing, encouraging, whatever it is you require. All you need do is accept and allow in flow and ease.

When you make flow and ease your normal way of being, you'll experience more joy and deep satisfaction. It may feel like floating on a cloud. This is the path to bliss, which is soul nirvana.

Just as with building your meditation muscles, you are now moving forward towards building bliss muscles.

While you're in the energy of bliss, it is more difficult for anyone or anything to upset your applecart. You are metaphorically floating on the most beautiful sea of well being.

Having experienced soul nirvana, you will be highly motivated to make it your normal way of being, because it's, well... soul nirvana! (Wink)

In the beginning, your periods of bliss may be brief. If in the very moment you notice you have strayed from bliss you quickly make a course correction (usually that's new action), you will find it much easier to regain your footing and get right back on track.

Over time bliss will become the rule rather than the exception. You are, or soon will be, on your way to becoming an expert at sustaining bliss for extended periods of time. One day it will be a rarity to experience anything less. This is what your soul has long yearned for.

Now imagine millions of highly-evolved souls experiencing this state of bliss. Imagine... that's Earthtopia!

Namasté Dear Child

Day 16 Journal

_____

_____

_____

_____

_____

_____

_____

_____

_____

_____

Challenge Day 17

Metatron: This process has evolved in a most delightful way. Better than even we anticipated. Your eagerness for the task, your willingness to stretch yourself, the expansion you have experienced, and the way your expansion has positively impacted all those in your sphere of connection, is pure joy.

We thank you for your diligence on your own behalf and that of the planet. It is a fact that when a great enough number come together in common purpose, the resulting impact will be felt around the world.

Each participant is an important component in the master plan. Your efforts matter a great deal. Your commitment and dedication matter. By staying the course *you* are inspiring others.

They may not have been ready, or believed in themselves enough to join the first challenge; but because of you they may join a future challenge. Your efforts have opened doors of opportunity for the many.

Did you know when you began that your efforts would contribute to shifting the consciousness of the planet? Perhaps not at the third dimensional level, but your soul knew, and you wisely chose to honor the call.

This is the beginning of a movement far greater than any one person. It's a movement on a planetary scale. Long awaited, much anticipated, and it has arrived. *You* have arrived at this monumental moment in time.

Yes there are challenging times ahead, but you are fully capable of weathering them, *and* standing firm on your sturdy sea legs.

Transformation of this scale requires effort. Your effort over the past 16 days has begun the process of tempering you (like fine steel), for what is to come.

Having begun this grand adventure, our sincere hope is that you will continue; for yourself and for the planet. While the effort required *is* great, the reward is oh so sweet — Earthtopia!

We remain ever at your side, guiding, supporting, showing the way, and cheering you on in perhaps the greatest mission of your many lifetimes. This is the one you've been preparing for, and the reason you're here on the planet now; while a great many others chose to opt out through the nearest exit.

It is not a season for the faint of heart, rather it's one for the souls who have diligently prepared, who have weathered many a challenging lifetime to qualify for donning warrior gear in this present lifetime.

Yes warrior. Each and every one of you is a warrior for the cause of saving the Earth, and yourselves, as you facilitate a great shift of consciousness and the realization of the prophecy of Earthtopia.

It is the grandest time to be alive. Savor it. Your time has arrived and you don't want to miss a single, delicious moment. This is the stuff of which epic tales are told.

You could be living future volumes of mythology at this very moment. How's that for a mind-bending concept?

Debbra: Metatron erupts in a hearty belly laugh. It's clear he's greatly anticipating the cosmic wave of transformation and all that it entails.

Vision: Metatron in the guise of Captain Ahab on stormy seas as he battles the forces of darkness, represented by the whale (Moby Dick).

DEBBRA: METATRON HAS DEPARTED LEAVING ME TO ponder this vision.

I thought Ahab was the bad guy in that story. This is confusing. Why would Metatron cast himself in the role of the bad guy? I get the distinct impression this is a message about illusions, things not being as they seem. We must go deeper to find the truth...

METATRON: THERE IS NEITHER GOOD NOR BAD. There are just choices and the consequences of those choices along your soul journey.

When you get caught up in assigning labels (judging), you slip out of alignment with your soul. The wise choice is: you take care of you and let others be responsible for themselves. Remember every person is a Divine soul, perfect in the eyes of Creator (no matter how flawed they appear).

When you're in alignment, you are filled to overflowing with love of self and the world. When everyone is in alignment, chaos and lawlessness are replaced by peace and harmony. That is the promise of Earthtopia.

Day 17 Journal

_____

_____

_____

_____

_____

_____

_____

_____

_____

_____

Challenge Day 18

Metatron: Slow and easy wins the race. Remain calm, centered and focused. Do not allow the drama of others to upset your applecart. Neither get sucked into the chaos that seems to become more pervasive every day.

Create your own protective bubble (Link p. 135), empower yourself to stand apart from the sturm and drang of the unawakened. They will be feeling more pressure, more angst, and more fear as their world shifts, and they are ill equipped to adapt.

You, Dear One, have been preparing. With your conditioned sea legs you'll weather the approaching storm. Do not fret when the unawakened are washed overboard, neither risk your well being saving them from their own folly. Remember it is their choice to remain in disempowered energy.

When it is their time they will depart, that is the way of things. They made choices that led to this eventuality, as you made choices to prepare yourself to surf the cosmic wave of transformation.

Now is not the time to be distracted by the consequences they manifested for themselves.

Breathe, relax, allow, focus… that is the mantra that will help sustain should your legs feel wobbly.

Pause, regroup, gather yourself up, and rejoin your soul sisters and brothers on your mutual journey of transformation.

You have long planned and awaited this time, now revel in the exhilaration of surfing expertly through the barrel of the wave.

Oh the celebrations you will enjoy when this chapter draws to a close and the next — Earthtopia — begins.

Some days you may have felt despair that you'd never reach this pinnacle. Yet deep down you kept the faith and that is what draws you here now.

Lightworkers standing together are an unstoppable force. Darkness must surrender, making way for the dawn of a new age so delicious you may want to pinch yourself to be sure it's real.

Yes, Dear Child, the goal is just over the horizon. Meanwhile, we recommend doubling down on self care in this lull before the storm. Prepare yourselves, your homes, your families (as best you can).

With a deep breath and release, allow those who are not in alignment to go their own way. Send them off with love, blessings and a light heart. It is all good and you may reconnect with them in a future lifetime if you choose.

Focus, focus, focus, on your vision of the golden era for humanity. It will take every lightworker standing in agreement and solidarity to crest that tsunami-level wave and surf into your bright future.

Trust, know, and believe that you *do* have what it takes to weather this storm. You *will* emerge on the other side to catch the first glimpse of your new world.

When that day arrives, much merriment will ensue. Tales will be told around ceremonial fires as you recount the great battle for *New Earth* while reveling in the deliciousness of your victory.

Some of you will record your stories for posterity. These stories will be passed down through the generations, who will read in wide-eyed wonder of the daring feats of their ancestors; marveling at their bravery and dedication to the cause from which they now benefit.

Debbra: Metatron, will people live longer in Earthtopia? We're hearing of people living well into their 100s. Does that mean this generation of lightworkers, or future generations?

Metatron: Some will live longer while others will choose to move on so that they might return in a fresh, new body.

Those who choose to extend their lives will find that their upgraded fourth dimensional bodies will possess more regenerative abilities. They will become stronger and more robust as they ascend towards ever higher vibrational frequency. All manner of new experiences await.

In an era of peace and harmony, your energy and focus will almost entirely shift to soul expansion as you explore possibilities that were previously unavailable. We will not go too far into the weeds, because some things are yet beyond your ability to comprehend. There will be time enough for more when you move up the next rung of the frequency ladder.

For now focus on the present. Follow your inspired ideas as you raise your consciousness higher in anticipation of the great shift. Stay on your course, find ways to incorporate joy and playfulness as often as possible. You have no idea how important those energies are to your journey. Indulge yourself. It's the wise choice.

Onward in faith, love, and light and you'll never walk alone. (Elvis singing *You'll Never Walk Alone* (Link p. 135))

Day 18 Journal

_____

_____

_____

_____

_____

_____

_____

_____

_____

_____

Challenge Day 19

Metatron: Day 19... ah yes, a momentous occasion. The final three days of the challenge.

Time is short and yet — is it?

Certainly, if you fall into the trap of focusing on the future rather than being present in each day, it may seem that way.

However, all you need do is bring your focus back to the now. Be present in each moment of *this* day.

Experience it fully. Notice the textures, nuances, sights, sounds, *feelings*.

Catalog it all as you relish your beingness. Using this approach will shift your perspective causing time to stretch. You will be amazed at how much more space you will have in a day when you shift into the *now* perspective.

As in all things, focus on what you already have and be glad in it, rather than pining for what has not yet arrived. That is a recipe to keep what you desire just out of reach, like the proverbial carrot on a stick.

Keep noticing what you don't have, and you'll notice more that you don't have. Time will accelerate and you'll become more frustrated because you seem unable to manifest even the small stuff.

Of course that is a misnomer because size has nothing to do with manifestation. It's all in your perspective. So we say: dial it in. Bask in appreciation for what you've already created, and allow us to do the heavy lifting to bring more of what you desire into your experience.

When you worry your desired manifestations, like a dog with a bone, you push away the very thing that you seek. Your noticing that it has not yet arrived creates ripples in the pond, pushing away what was nearly within reach.

Again we remind you: breathe, relax, allow, and focus on being fully present in your life, lest it pass you by in a blur. You've done this before and when that life was finished, you were quite put out with yourself for once more falling into the same old rut, like a broken record.

"When will I ever stop defeating myself?" You railed.

To that we reply: Now. Now. Now. Do it now! It's time and you really can. Slow down, be fully present and give yourself the gift of really "living" this life. You can thank us later. 😉

Transmission complete.

Day 19 Journal

_____

_____

_____

_____

_____

_____

_____

_____

_____

_____

_____

Challenge Day 20

Debbra: Hearing Joni Mitchell singing *Both Sides Now* (Link p. 135). Is that relevant to the message, Metatron?

Metatron: Of course.

Debbra: Are you referencing how there's so much we don't know?

Metatron: There is a great deal still unknown. People, places and events are in play. A great deal of free choice in the mix. We have a sense of what direction events will take. There's a broad framework in place. However, through your choices, each of you fill in the details.

This is why it's so important to come together with clarity and common purpose, because there is strength in numbers and the coming challenge will be great.

Gather together and bring friends. Spread the word to every corner of the planet so that those who have ears to hear will heed the call. Remember, it's vital to reach critical mass as soon as possible.

Yes, that is the energy of urgency you detect in my voice. There is much preparation yet to be completed. It's an all-hands-on-deck moment.

All of the energy, and intention you've previously put forth has served to set the wheels in motion. Now what's called for is a redoubling of effort as the time draws near.

Debbra: When you say draws near, are you talking about years or months?

Silence.

Can you answer that question?

Metatron: No, not at this time. Even we do not have that information as the timeline shifts depending upon your efforts. We feel it is imminent, but we also have a different perspective on time than you. At this point it's likely years rather than months; but less than 10, more than 10, it's too soon to say.

We ask for your patience and diligence. Witness the progress you have made during this challenge. Now imagine multiplying your numbers in a 700 x 700 expansion. That's what is needed to move the needle forward towards the great shift.

We've observed an acceleration of awakening amongst light-workers. As that expansion gains momentum, it will act as a catalyst awakening yet more lightworkers.

Do not underestimate the fear which has caused many to live as if they wore blinders; unaware of the destiny they chose for this lifetime; blocked by multi-layered past-life traumas.

You will be the way showers for them, demonstrating why it's important to release karmic baggage and how they can rapidly do so through this meditation process.

Imagine their delight at throwing off their burdens and finally understanding they are magnificent souls come to fulfill a grand purpose.

When you role model living in a state of alignment and joy, they will be inspired to join you on the transformational journey to facilitate Earthtopia.

As your numbers grow, it will become easier for them to have faith and confidence — to allow for the possibility of soul nirvana.

Imagine a time when the majority of Earth's inhabitants are joined in the singular purpose of raising their vibrational frequency through consciousness expansion. That's Earthtopia!

The more who join the cause, the more who will want to. This is why it's a psychic, rather than physical, battle. Upon awakening, more souls will tap into their intuitive/psychic abilities, remember the truth of who they are, and their role in the great shift.

There are many who are weary of the same old injustice, corruption, malfeasance, bigotry, and hatred. They are ready for a better way, but perhaps do not believe it possible. They have been beaten down for so many lifetimes it has become normal.

Day 20 Journal

_____

_____

_____

_____

_____

_____

_____

_____

_____

_____

_____

Challenge Day 21

Debbra: Ok Metatron, today is Lion's Gate. What message do you have to share on this last momentous day of your challenge?

Metatron: Singing — Ta ra ra boom de ay

The celebration is in progress. On this most auspicious occasion of the very first group to undertake this challenge we are throwing a gargantuan party. All of the teams have come together to have a rip roaring time. You deserve it and so do we!

You may join us at the party if you like. It will be *happening* for a day, maybe more. There is tremendous exhilaration at achieving this monumental milestone. We encourage you to spend some time celebrating yourself as well.

Also it would be wise to take some time to process how you feel about the experience.

What did you learn? How has it changed you? What do you intend to do next?

Will you continue some sort of regular meditation practice?

If you decide to continue, we encourage you to mix things up. Don't go all rigid about how you *should* meditate, because as this experience has demonstrated, all those *shoulds* do you a great disservice.

Also feel free to skip the timer (unless your schedule requires it). Just be meditative for as long as the session flows.

After you complete today's meditation and have some time to process, you may want to review your journal. We expect you'll be astonished at how your experience has evolved since Day 1.

You are not the same person who began this challenge. Your soul is more firmly seated in your body. Your oneness with self has, and is, expanding. Your perspective of self and your world has shifted (even if just a smidge).

We wish to honor and thank you for your commitment to this cause. We *see* you and stand at your side, today and every day.

We eagerly anticipate your further expansion. If you think you feel great today, just wait! This is one level of connection, more await.

Your work has opened more doors of opportunity than you likely imagined were possible. Now you understand that everything is possible! It's up to you to decide what you wish to create, then set about doing just that.

Greatness is within you. It always was. We hope you've gotten at least a glimpse at what you're capable of.

If not, know that you will. Just keep going. Never give up on yourself, because we surely never will.

We encourage you to gather together. Support one another. Share, ask questions. In this way you will facilitate one another's expansion. That is a beautiful vision we will hold in our hearts.

Now that you've fast tracked your ascension, continue looking for the magic in daily life and expect miracles. You are now firmly grounded in the ways and means of both.

We want you to know beyond a shadow of a doubt, from the top of your head to the tips of your toes what a magnificent service you have given yourself and the world.

Even more joy, wonder, and delight await you along your chosen path. Nurture that powerful spark within, guard and keep it burning so that you may use it to light the inner spark of others who are just beginning their journey.

There are a great many souls who have yet to set forth on their awakening journey. As you share with them, and they share with others, momentum will build. Soon this movement will spread across the globe, lighting inner spark flames from one person to another.

It really can be that simple.

Keep your eyes on the goal.

Do what feeds your soul.

Share and move ever onward until your days are done, and you can depart this life with the deep satisfaction of knowing that *you* were a part of something bigger than any one person. *You* were a primary facilitator of the evolution to Earthtopia.

Yes that will create a whole lot of great karma, but even more importantly, you will have cleared the slate of a boatload of old trauma and its associated karma. You will have finally stared down the fear demon that has haunted you, lo these many lifetimes, and you will have vanquished it!

Henceforth you will carry in your Akashic Records the designation of *Fear Slayer* (amongst your other accomplishments).

THIS is a consequential lifetime that will pay dividends through many lifetimes to come.

Debbra: Any more accolades or wise guidance Metatron? What is the most important thought you want to convey.

Metatron: Never forget how very loved you are. From the depths of the deepest ocean, to the peaks of the highest mountain, across the vast expanse of the largest desert, and spanning the circumference of Earth herself. All of them put together and more. That is how much your Creator, and your team, love and adore you. That is true today and all the days unto infinity.

In other words, the depth of love for you defies measurement! Know it. Feel it. Trust it. Believe it. Because it is Divine truth.

Amen.

Signing off for now, but remember we're just a whisper away. Don't forget to call — often would be grand.

Much love and many blessings to you Beloved.

Day 21 Journal

_____

_____

_____

_____

_____

_____

_____

_____

_____

_____

_____

Afterword

Congratulations on completing Metatron's challenge! Now is the time to sit back and reflect upon your experience. What have you learned? How have you changed?

Will you continue your new meditation practice? I sure hope so because it truly is a game changer — even if you don't practice daily.

If you haven't already, grab the reader bonus book (https://AkashaUnleashed.com/lightworkers-path), which contains (at the time of this writing) nine more messages from Metatron that were delivered at weekly intervals after the challenge.

Should there be more messages in this series I will add them to the ebook and notify you via email so that you can grab an updated copy.

I hope that you'll share what you've learned with others, because as Metatron says: we need to reach critical mass in the number of lightworkers in order to realize the prophecy of Earthtopia.

We can speed up the timeline through our efforts. I don't know about you, but I'm sure ready. Let's do this!

About the Author

Debbra Lupien, is a Spiritual Teacher, Author, and Voice of the Akashic Records.

She previously authored the international best-selling book, *Akasha Unleashed: The Missing Manual To You,* which has become a catalyst for personal transformation across the globe.

Debbra believes the holy grail of your soul journey is to find what feeds your soul — and DO IT. Wise souls avail themselves of the shortcut found in the Akashic Records. In addition to writing, she regularly shares channeled messages, meditations, and spiritual lessons on her YouTube channel.

Connecting & Links

Debbra is available for private **readings**, **speaking** engagements, **workshops**, and live **channeled events**. Reach out to her through her website: AkashaUnleashed.com or via email: Answers@AkashaUnleashed.com

You'll find **All Links** referenced throughout this workbook at: https://akashaunleashed.com/lightworkers-path

Also by Debbra Lupien

Akasha Unleashed: The Missing Manual to You

Co-Authored Books:

The Wellness Universe Guide to Complete Self-Care: 25 Tools for Stress Relief

Unscripted: How Women Thrive in Life, Business, and Relationships

Conscious Creators Magazine: Discover the Secrets of Awakened Women

Notes

Notes

Printed in Poland
by Amazon Fulfillment
Poland Sp. z o.o., Wrocław

30581690R00081